Webster's Gold

Georgia A. Johnson, M. D.

First published 1990, by Georgia A. Johnson, M. D.

Georgia A. Johnson Publishing Company
P. O. Box 4796, East Lansing, Michigan 48826

Printed in the United States

ISPN# 0-9626450-1-X

Library of Congress Catalogue Number: 89-92739

Main entries under title:

1	Michigan History	1834-1850
2	Gold Rush letters	1850-1856
3	Webster genealogy	
4	Stebbins genealogy	
5	Burroughs genealogy	

Table of Contents

Introduction

The main subjects of this account, Lyman and Dimis Webster, left Conway, Massachusetts, with their five children in 1834 to settle in Kent County, Michigan Territory. They were among the adventuresome who would leave their New England homes to settle along the Grand River Valley of central Michigan. Lyman Webster was an eighth generation descendant of Governor John Webster, the fifth governor of the state of Connecticut, 1656-1657. It is worthy of note that Noah Webster, the famous lexicographer and author of the *American Dictionary of the English Language*, was a sixth generation descendant of the Governor.

I have in my possession original land deeds, letters from the California gold rush regions, and copies of court documents pertaining to the Lyman Webster family of Clinton County, Michigan. These materials and their transcriptions will constitute the major portion of this text.

In addition, I have included a letter written to Dimis Webster, Lyman's wife, from her cousin, Alan Bradford of Haydenville, Massachusetts, and several pages of genealogical data concerning her family, the Stebbins family.

Mrs. Jean Anderson Openlander graciously permitted me to include copies of a daguerreotype and of photographs of members of the Webster family. Mrs. Openlander is the great-granddaughter of Lyman's son, Edwin Dewey Webster. Data was also obtained from county histories and other resources too numerous to mention here.

I transcribed Lyman's letters verbatim, and in order to maintain the authenticity of them made no attempt to correct spelling errors, to capitalize proper names and pronouns, or to add punctuation marks. Generally Lyman did not leave a space between sentences or capitalize the first word of each sentence. I did add an extra space between what appeared to be complete sentences to facilitate the reading of the letters. Where I could not decipher a word I left a blank.

Thanks go to Dr. John W. Ball for his consultant and photographic services.

Lyman Webster

Lyman Webster was one of nine children of Jacob and Lovina Hemingway of Conway, Massachusetts. Jacob was a farmer and held the office of highway surveyor about 1814. Lyman Webster married Dimis Stebbins in 1825. His occupation was that of farmer. Their five older children, Nancy, Theodore, Edwin Dewey, Lovina, and Louisa, were all born in Conway, Massachusetts. The next two children, Caroline and Mary Jane, were born in Ionia, Michigan, and the remaining three, Charles, Helen, and Henry, in Essex Township, Clinton County, Michigan.

Documented events of Lyman Webster's life

A reference to Lyman appears in Volume 5 of the *Kent County Michigan Land Records* page 1426: Webster, Lyman, Res. Kent Co., grantor. Abrams S. Wadsworth, Res. Ionia Co., Mich. grantee. Convey land on Sec. 1, Grand Rapids Twp. Liber 24, pg. 15, Oct. 30, 1834.

A biography of Henry W. Webster in the *History of Clinton and Shiawassee Counties, Michigan*, 1891, page 970, states that his father, Lyman, owned 160 acres of land now included in Grand Rapids.

Ione Anderson, a great-granddaughter of Lyman Webster, in a booklet entitled "Here Come the Yankees from Massachusetts," 1970, recorded additional information. In 1834, Lyman and his family arrived in Kent County, Michigan, where they erected a sawmill. They soon moved to Ionia County, where the oldest children attended the public school. The children walked to the Grand River, where an Indian squaw awaited them in her canoe. She paddled them across the river to the school house. Lyman was called "Maquah" by his Indian neighbors because of his heavy black beard.

In the book, *Memorials of the Grand River Valley*, page 51, under the heading, "The next year, 1835, brought more accessions. . .," was the statement, "Lyman Webster bought out Joel Guild, but did not stay long" in Ionia.

The *History of Ionia and Montcalm Counties, Michigan*, provides further information: George B. Porter, Governor of the Michigan Territory, in 1833 chose commissioners to locate the county seats in Ionia, Clinton and Kent counties. The commissioners decided to locate the Ionia county seat in the town of

Ionia in the North 1/2 of Section 19, Township 7N, Range 6W, on the lands of Samuel Dexter.

Lyman Webster was one of 32 citizens of Ionia County who petitioned Steven T. Mason, the acting governor of the Michigan Territory, to honor the decision of the commissioners. The petition was dated February 11, 1835. An executive proclamation confirming the commissioners' report was issued in 1835 or 1836.

Lyman was elected highway commissioner at a special Ionia township meeting May 12, 1835, and was re-elected to the same post April 4, 1836.

The Federal Land Patents, Kent County, Michigan, page 67, lists Lyman Webster as purchaser of the SE quarter of Section 25, Township 7N, Range 11W, in Grand Rapids Township on September 28, 1836. The 160-acre plat cost $1.25 per acre for a total sale price of $200. On August 1, 1837, Lyman Webster's purchase was patented. Plat map of Grand Rapids Township, Kent County, Michigan, 1841 (Exhibit 1).

A warranty deed of April 24, 1837, (Exhibits 2a and 2b) gives evidence that Lyman and Dimis Webster sold to Joseph W. Brown and Robert S. Parks a certain parcel of land in Ionia County, namely: the W half of the NW quarter of Section 20 in Township 7N, Range 6W, containing 80 acres.

September 2, 1837 (Exhibit 3), Dimis and Lyman Webster purchased a portion of the land they had sold in April, 1837. The deed reveals that they purchased the following land from Robert S. and Sarah Parks and Larson L. and Emily Warner: the W half of the W half of the NW quarter of Section 20, of 40 acres, and 6-8 acres in Section 19. This land is now within the city limits of Ionia, being a portion of the Warner addition annexed to the city on August 25, 1841. Interestingly the land purchased from Samuel Dexter in December 1833 for the site of the "Ionia County Seat" was also located in Section 19, being the N half of Section 19, Township 7N, Range 6W.

An article of agreement was made November 4, 1837 (Exhibit 4), by which Chester Walbridge sold to Lyman Webster the E half of the SW quarter of Section 25. Township 8N, Range 3W, 80 acres of land in Clinton County, Michigan. This parcel of land was assigned successively to Wandaugon, Lebanon, Bengal and Essex Townships. A photocopy of a map of Wandaugon (Essex) Township of Clinton County, 1818-1841, has the names Webster and Stebbins written at the sites of their homesteads in Sections 25 and 26 respectively. Map

(Exhibit 5) courtesy of the Maple Rapids Public Library, Maple Rapids, Michigan.

In 1838 Clinton County's 3 townships were administratively attached to Shiawassee County. Wandaugon did not report the results of its April election. Lebanon township, formerly Wandaugon, held its election in April, 1839. Lyman was elected Director of Poor and Overseer of Highways, while his brother-in-law, Chauncey M. Stebbins, was elected Assessor.

Act No. 58, Section 10, approved by the Michigan Legislature on March 19, 1840, stated that all that part of the County of Clinton designated in the United States survey as Townships 7 and 8N of Range 3W be organized into a township by the name of Bengal, and that the first township meeting therein be held at the house of James Sowle, Jr., in said township.

In accordance with the above act, the first Bengal township meeting was held on April 18, 1840. Lyman Webster was elected to the offices of Highway Commissioner, Justice of the Peace and Overseer of the Poor.

The second township meeting was held at the home of Sylvester Stephens, April 23, 1841. Lyman Webster was elected to the office of Inspector of Schools and his brother-in-law, Chauncey M. Stebbins, to the office of Assessor. Lyman's name was returned as a member of the petit jury and Chauncey's as a member of the grand jury. At the same meeting it was voted that the next township meeting be held at the home of Chauncey M. Stebbins.

The third township meeting was held in April 1842 at the home of Chauncey M. Stebbins who was elected Supervisor. Lyman was elected Clerk.

On April 3, 1843, the township meeting was held in the barn of James Sowle, Jr. The election was set aside, for the reason that the north half of Bengal, in which most of the elected officers resided, had been set off and erected as the township of Essex by an act of the legislature approved March 9, 1843. A special election was then ordered in each township. That in Essex was held April 21, and in Bengal April 26, 1843.

Lyman was named Clerk of Essex Township in 1844 and Highway Commissioner in 1847.

The Circuit Court of the County of Clinton was held in Dewitt during the regular term commencing May 7, 1841. On this day the Honorable Charles W. Whipple, a justice of the Supreme Court and presiding judge of the Circuit and Joseph Seaver and Hiram Wilcox, associate judges of the County of Clinton, were present. There being no prosecuting attorney, the court appointed Calvin C. Parks to perform the duties of the office during the term. The grand jury came in, presented sundry indictments and was discharged. The case of the People vs. Lyman Webster, for embezzlement, was called, and on motion of the prosecuting attorney it was ordered that the prisoner enter in recognizance of himself in the amount of three hundred dollars and a surety in the sum of two hundred dollars consideration for his appearance at the next term of court. There being no further business, the court adjourned.

At the second term of the Clinton County Circuit Court, in October, 1841, the first petit jury was called. Lyman Webster was named as one of the jurors.

The following is a listing of Clinton County records which refer to the proceedings of the county against Lyman Webster 1840-1842.

Aug. 3, 1840	Summons to Alonzo Brewster, to appear as witness
*Oct. 3, 1840	Deposition of Ephriam Utley (Exhibit 6)
Oct. 3, 1840	Complaint of Ephriam Utley
Oct. 3, 1840	Warrant for arrest of Lyman Webster
*Oct. 12, 1840	Testimony of Ephriam Utley and Alonzo Brewster (Exhibit 7)
Oct. 12, 1840	Bond of Lyman Webster and David Scott for appearance at Circuit Court
May 8, 1841	Bench warrant for Lyman Webster
*May 8, 1841	True Bill of Indictment by the Circuit Court (Exhibit 8)
May 8, 1841	Recognizance by Lyman Webster and surety
May 8, 1841	Warrant to secure appearance of Lyman Webster Oct. 9, 1841
Sept. 20, 1841	Notice to appear as witness to Ephriam Utley and Alonzo Brewster
*Oct. 9, 1841	Verdict of Petit Jury (Exhibit 9)
Oct. 9, 1841	Recognizance of Lyman Webster and surety
May 6, 1842	Recognizance of Lyman Webster and surety

Exhibit 6 (Oct. 3, 1840)

State of Michigan   Ephraim H Utley being Duly
Clinton County ss   Sworn deposeth and saith that
on or About the 20 day of July last he did Deliver
to Lyman Webster several county orders to Deliver
to Different individuals in the town of Lebanon
and that the said Lyman Webster has fraudently
converted two of said orders to his own useas this affiant varyly believes
Sworn and subscribed this 3 day of Oct 1840
William A. Hewit Justice of the Peace

Exhibit 7 (Oct. 12, 1840)

Witness on the part of the presentation
Ephraim H. Utley sworn as complainant Sayeth that some time
in July last thinks near the twentyth he the deponent
Delivered to Lyman Webster Several county orders to deliver
to the owners to whom they were given as of said orders was given
to John P. Miller of sixteen Dollars and one to Alonzo D.
Brewster of Eight dollars further sayeth that he saw said
Webster some time after and spoke to him about the said orders
and said Webster said that he had sent word to the owners
by doctor Beckworth but had not sent the order but would
send them soon. Further Sayeth that he
Alonzo D. Brewster sworn saith that he
left with Mr Utley some sertiffictoes to be audited
and he called on Mr Utley for the orders some time in September
last said Utley found by examing his Records that the
accounts had been audited but could not tell whose the
orders was but thought that he had sent them to him by
Mr Webster but might be mistaken and said Utley was to
ascertain where the said order was if he could and write
to him as soon as he found where the order was Saith
he called on Mr Utley again the first of October and said Utley

Said the reason why he did not write was because
he had seen Mr Webster and Mr Webster said that he had
sent word to Mr Brewster by Mr Beckworth that he had
the orders Ready for him he had Received one order of
sixteen dollars given to him by Mr Hall of Lyons
one of Sixteen Dollars given to John P. Miller and one of Eight Dollars
given to Alonzo D. Brewster he found in the country treasurers
office paid for He Sayeth that he never gave any order
to any person to Draw pay on said order and the he nor
said Miller has not Received any pay of the Same

(back of page)

The People
    vs
Lyman Webster
Embezzlement

Exhibit 8 (May 8, 1841)

State of Michigan
Clinton County ss Circuit Court for said
                  County of the Term of May
One thousand eight Hundred and forty one
Clinton County ss
                  The grand Jurors of the
People of the State of Michigan inquiring in
and for the body of the County of Clinton
on their oath present that Lyman Webster
late of the Township of DeWitt in the County of Clin
=ton aforesaid on the fifteenth day of June in
the year one thousand eight hundred and forty
_____at the Township aforesaid in the County
aforesaid then and there being employed
by Ephraim H. Utley Chairman of the Board of County

Commissioners within and for said County of Clinton
to take possession of Certain Evidences of Debt commonaly
called county orders and did then and there employ
him the Said Lyman Webster to Carry and deliver
the said Evidence of Debt to one Alonzo D. Brewster
of said County of Clinton which evidence of Debt
are in Substanced following to wit=

Clinton County

no 56   10 April 1840
     Due John P. Miller or Bearer Sixteen dollars
payable at the Treasurer office of Clinton County and
Receivable for Taxes
     By order of the Board of County Commissioners
$16.00   (signed) Seth P. Marvin Clerk

no 57   10 April 1840
Due Alonzo D. Brewster or Bearer   Eight
dollars payable at the Treasurer office of Clinton
County and Received for taxes
     By order of the Board of County Commissioners
$8.00   (signed) Seth P. Marvin Clerk
The same being the property of said County of
Clinton of the value of twenty-four Dollars
and the said Lyman Webster by virture of his
said Employment - did then and there and
whilst - he was so employed as aforesaid Receive
and take into his possession said Evidence
of debt commonly called county orders described
as aforesaid of the value aforesaid for on in
the service of the County - aforesaid and the
said Evidence did Embezzle and so these
jurors aforesaid upon their oath aforesaid
do say that the said Lyman Webster then
and there in manner and form aforesaid the
said evidence of debt the property of the Said

County of Clinton for the Said County of
Clinton Feloniously did steal, take and
carry away contrary to the form of the Statute
and against the Peace and dignity of the
people of the State of Michigan

And the Grand Jurors aforesaid upon
their oath aforesaid do further present that
on the twenty fifth day of July in the year
one thousand eight hundred and forty at the Town
=ship of Dewitt in the County of Clinton aforesaid
Ephraim H. Utley did intrust The said Lyman
Webster the said Lyman Webster then and there offering
his Service as agent for John P. Miller and
Alonzo D. Brewster with evidencies of Debt commonly
called County orders being obligations against this said
County of Clinton signed by Seth A. Marvin as Clerk
of the Board of County Commissioners of the said County
of Great value to wit of the value of twenty four
Dollars with Directions to the said Lyman Webster
to carry and deliver the same to the said Alonzo
D. Brewster which he the said Lyman Webster
promised well and faithfully to perform and that
the said Lyman Webster late of the Township aforesaid
in the County aforesaid agent as aforesaid afterwards
to wit on the day and year last aforesaid at the
Township aforesaid in the County aforesaid in
violation of good faith and contrary to the
purpose so as aforesaid specified unlawfully and
feloniously did embezzle and unlawfully
did convert to to his own use and benefit the said
Evidences of Debt specified as aforesaid so to him
Intrusted as aforesaid and the said evidence of Debt
from the said John P. Miller and
Alonzo Brewster did feloniously steal take
and carry away contrary to the form of the statute

and against the peace and dignity of the people
of the State of Michigan

And the Grand Jurors aforesaid upon their
oath aforesaid do further present Lyman Webster
late in the Township of Dewitt in the county of Clinton
on the twenty fifth day of July in the year one
thousand eight hundred and forty at the Township
aforesaid and county aforesaid two obligations
as evidences of Debt (commonally called county orders)
against the County of Clinton for the payment of
twenty four Dollars and the value of twenty
four Dollars the property of John P Miller
and Alonzo D Brewster then and there being found the
said Sum of twenty four Dollars Secured and pay=
able by and upon the said obligation being then
and there due and unsatisfied to the Said John
P Miller and Alonzo D Brewster - Feloniously did
steal take and carry away against the form
of the statue in such case made and provided and
against the peace and dignity of the people of
the State of Michigan   Calvin C Parks
                               Acting Pros atty

(back of second page)

Circuit Court Clinton County

The People
     vs
Lyman Webster

A True Bill
Daniel Ferguson
    Foreman
Exhibit Filed

in open Court this
8th May 1841
Seth P. Marvin   Clerk
C. C. Parks   acting Pros atty

Exhibit 9 (Oct. 9, 1841)

Guilty on the first part

Barney Allen
Jesse Olmsted
Smith Parker
Calvin Barber
Reuben Rogers
Darius B Cranson
Richard Lewis
F W Cronkhite
Henry Jipson
Ransom Reed
G A Merrihew
B(Benjamin) Merrihew

(back of page)

The People
    vs
Lyman Webster

Verdict of Petit Jury

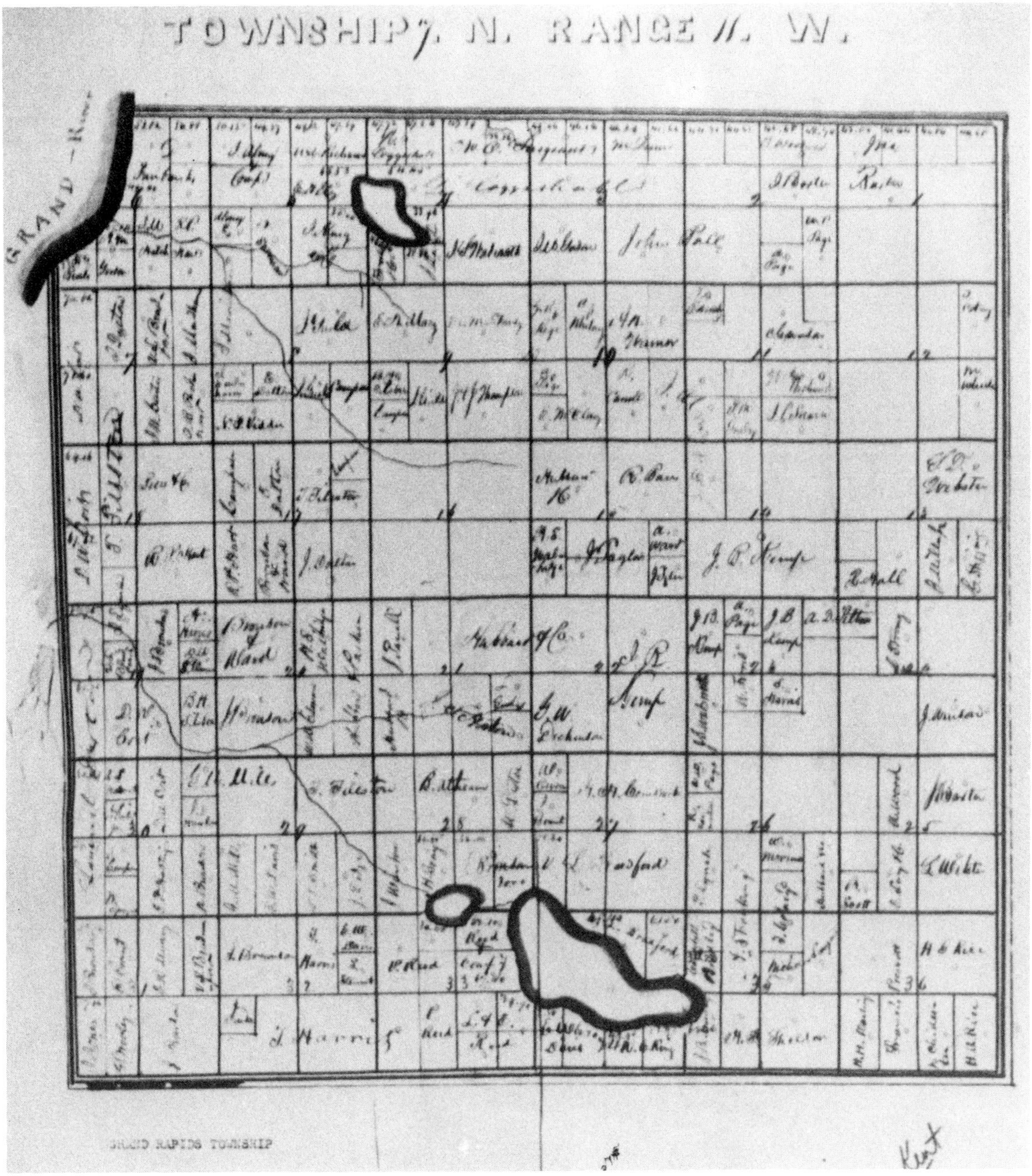
TOWNSHIP 7. N. RANGE 11. W.
GRAND RIVER
John Ball
GRAND RAPIDS TOWNSHIP
Kent

Exhibit 1

Know all Men by these Prese

the County of [Fonda?] in the State of [...]
Four thousand Seven Hundred [...]
Parties

acknowledge, do by these presents, give, grant, bargain, sell an

Three heirs and as

aforesaid bounded and descr

Quarter of Section Twenty [...]
No. Six (6) West, containing [...]

Together with all the privileges and appurtenances, to the s
ises to the said *Joseph W. Brown and Ro*
and behoof forever. And *he* the said *Lyman & [...]*
covenant with said *Joseph W. Brown & Robert [...]*
afore-granted premises; that they are free from all incumbran
their heirs and assigns
administrators shall WARRANT AND DEFEND the same
assigns forever against the lawful demands of all persons.

In Witness Whereof, *we* have hereunto set *o[...]*
thousand eight hundred and thirty- *Seven.*

Signed, Sealed and Delivered, }
in presence of }

Jacob Gilman

Thomas Cornell

Wm [...]

Exhibit 2(a)

That *We Lyman Webster and Dimis his wife of Jonia in* ____ party of the first part, in consideration of ____ Dollars, to *us* paid by *Joseph H. Brown and Robert S.* party of the second part, the receipt whereof *we* do hereby ____ unto the said party of the second part ____ certain parcel of land, situate in *in the Town County and State* follows, to wit: *Being the West half of the Northwest* ____ *in Township No. Seven (7) North of Range* ____ *acres be the same or less.*

____ in any wise appertaining and belonging: TO HAVE AND TO HOLD the above granted prem- ____ *or Packer their* ____ heirs and assigns, to ____ and their use ____ for ____ heirs, executors and administrators, do ____ *their* heirs and assigns, that *we are* lawfully seized in fee of the ____ *we* have good right to sell and convey the same to the said *Brown & Packer* as aforesaid; and that *we* will, and *our* heirs, executors ____ said *Brown & Packer their* ____ heir ____

____ and seals this ____ day of *April* in the year of our Lord one ____

Lyman Webster [Seal]

Dimis S. Webster [Seal]

15

State of Michigan
Ionia County ss— At Ionia in said County on the 24th day of April 1837 personally came before me the undersigned one of the justices of the peace within & for said County Lyman Mosted & Dinis his wife well known to me to be the persons who executed the within deed and acknowledged that they freely executed the same for the uses & purposes therein expressed — And the said Dinis being examined privately and apart from her husband acknowledged that she freely signed Sealed & delivered the same without fear or compulsion from him —

Thomas Cornell Justice of the peace

Exhibit 2 (b)
reverse side
of deed

17

This Indenture,

Lord one thousand eight hundred and Thirty Seven
Lawson S Warner & Emily his wife,
of Ionia, Michigan

that the said parties of the first part, for and in consideration of

confessed and acknowledged, have granted, bargained, sold, re
said part of the
and described as follows to wit; Th
tion (20) Twenty- also the un
follow, to wit: begining at a
teen and (20) Twenty- thence
to Grand River - thence
River crosses the line betwee
North to place of beginn
the same more or Less all in
the Grand River district - a
Ty, to the said Lyman Wester

TOGETHER with all and singular, the hereditaments and
mainder and remainders, rents, issues and profits thereof; and
first part, either in Law or Equity, of, in and to the above
To have and to hold the said premises as above described, wit
ever. And the said parties of the first part, for them
agree, to and with the said party of the second part, His
well seized of the premises above conveyed, as of a good, sure
above bargained premises, in the quiet and peaceable possessi
every person or persons, lawfully claiming or to claim the who

In Witness Whereof, the said parties of the first part have he

Sealed and delivered
in presence of

Hampton Rich

Chs Smith

Exhibit 3

18

Second   day of September   in the ye   of our

BETWEEN Robt. S. Parks & Sarah his wife and

Ionia Co. Michigan of the first part, and Lyman Webster

of the second part, WITNESSETH

um of Three Thousand Seven Hundred Dollars

s in hand paid, by the said party of the second part, the receipt whereof is hereby

ased, iened and confirmed, and by these presents do grant, bargain, sell, remise, release,

Conte parcel or pice kno

st half of the West half of the North west quarter of

vided half of a certain fraction of Land described as

t, being the quarter post between Section (19) Nine-

ning East Thirty two Rods — thence running South

y, along said River to a point where said

ec. (19) Nineteen and (20) Twenty = thence

Supposed to contain Six or Eight acres be

n (7) Seven North & Range (6) Six West in

y reserving an acre in the above mentioned (Eigh=

tenances thereunto belonging, in anywise appertaining; and the reversion and reversions, re=

e estate, right, title, interest, claim, or demand whatsoever of the said parties of the

d premises with the said hereditaments and appurtenances.

ppurtenances, unto the said party of the second part, and to His heirs and afsigns, for=

, their   heirs, executors and administrators, do covenant, grant, bargain and

nd afsigns, that at the time of the ensealing and delivery of these presents, they were

t, absolute and indefeasible estate of inheritance in the Law, in fee simple; and that the

he said party of the second part His   heirs and afsigns, against all and

y part thereof We will forever **Warrant and Defend.**

t their hand and seal the day and year first above written.

R. S. Parks — [S.S.]

Sarah N. Parks [S.S.]

Lawson S. Warner [S.S.]

Emily Warner [S.S.]

Articles of agreement made and concluded this 4th day of November 1837 Between Chester Walbridge of the first part and Lyman Webster of the Second part. Witnesseth — The party of the first part agrees to Sell and Convey by Good and Sufficient deed the following Land being the East half of the South West quarter of Section No Twenty five Town No 8 N R 3 West Containing Eighty acres in Clinton County, State of Michigan State according to the returns thereof by the Surveyor General of the United States be the Same more or less for the full Sum of five hundred dollars with interest from this date payable as follows the whole Sum and Intrest to be paid by the party of the Second part by the first day of April 1838 if Said party of the Second part Shall Recive his pay on a note he holds against Charles Hubbell for $600 and Endorsed by C A Trobridge & Parks & Warren but in case the party of the Second part Shall not Recive his pay on Said note he then binds himself to pay the full Sum of five hundred dollars with Intrest on the first day of October 1838 and the party makeing default Shall pay unto the other party the full Sum of five hundred dollars ~~damages~~ as Lequidated damages in witness whereof the parties have hereunto Set their hands and Seals the day and year above written

in presence of

Free Smith

Toledo Nov 4 1837
Lucas Co. Ohio.

Chester Walbridge (L.S.)

Lyman Webster (S.S.)

Exhibit 4

20

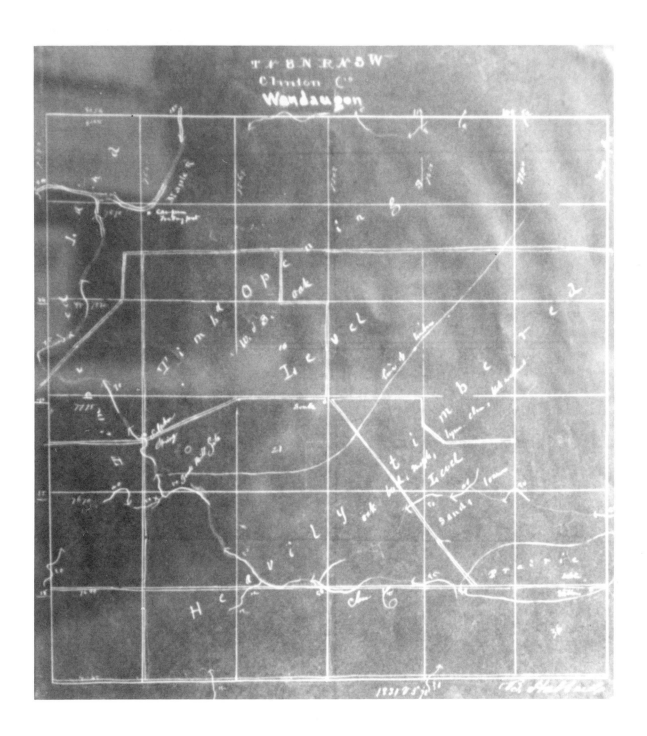

Exhibit 5

Lyman Webster's life changed abruptly in 1850 when he left Michigan for the gold fields. What we know of the remainder of his life appears in twelve letters he wrote back to his family and in three other documents; these letters and documents are briefly noted here and are also represented as exhibits in a later section of this book.

1. April 26, 1850
Letter from Lyman Webster from Chicago to his son, Edwin Dewey Webster, Essex, Clinton County, Michigan
Lyman and his companions waited three days at the mouth of the Grand River at Grand Haven, Michigan, for a steamer to Milwaukee, Wisconsin. A steamer, The Champion, made weekly trips between Milwaukee and Grand Haven. Lyman planned to leave Chicago for Saint Louis, Missouri, in a few days.

2. May 11, 1850 (Photostat, p. 26)
Lyman directed a letter to Mrs. E. D.Webster from Saint Joseph, Missouri. Saint Joseph and Independence, Missouri, were towns where wagon trains assembled and argonauts launched their overland journeys to the gold fields of California.

3. December 8, 1850
Lyman's letter to Dimis Webster from Hangtown, California
Hangtown (Placerville) was the site of dry diggings in El Dorado County, California, and was founded February 18, 1850. The northern border of the county is the middle fork of the American River. Just north of Hangtown is Coloma, where, when gold was found at Sutter's Mill in 1849, the Gold Rush began.

4. January 4, 1851 (Photostat, p. 28)
This letter was sent from El Dorado County and directed to Mr. Hiram Richmond, of Essex, Clinton County, Michigan
Lyman complained of the lack of rain and his company's inability to wash the dirt they had piled up. He mentioned travelling on the Humboldt River for 6-700 miles, (actually 300 miles), and reported that the water was like alkali. The Humboldt or Saint Mary's River has its source at Elko, Nevada, and is a respectable river for 250 miles; then it diminishes for 50 miles and finally disap-

pears into the earth at the Sink. The soil along its banks is permeated by alkali, sodium and potassium carbonates leeched from plant ashes, that blistered the skin and made the water unpalatable where the flow was sluggish. The water of the Humboldt could be made potable by the addition of cream of tartar. Travellers on the Overland Trail to California followed the river across much of present-day Nevada. They then crossed 50 miles of desert to Carson City (Ragtown), Nevada, crossed the Sierra Nevada mountains, and descended in the Sacramento Valley's gold fields.

5. November 20, 1851, Niles, Michigan
Letter from S.W. Griffins to Mrs. Dimis Webster regarding draft of $300 from Lyman.

6. February 15, 1852 Sunit River
Lyman stated that his company of three men were dry digging in Kioty Ravine and were hoping for rain to wash out their piled-up dirt. They were awaiting a machine to work on their grant. Kiote diggins were mining sites northwest of Nevada City, California. The word Kiote was given to the process of tunneling into the hills and shoring the tunnels with timbers, or Kiote.

7. April 25, 1852 Sunit Diggins
Lyman and a Dutchman went on a prospecting trip into the mountains (Sierra Nevada) and planned to form a company of 12 men. As the water supply had failed, Lyman said the company would soon be moved to Turttle Hill on the south fork of the north fork of the American River.

8. May 31, 1852
Mr. M. Nodges sent a letter from San Francisco to Mrs. Webster notifying her that Lyman was working at Mt. Greyby about eighty miles from Sacramento.

9. June 10, 1852
Lyman's letter from Turttle Hill stated that he sent $200 to pay for the west eighty (acres). His company of 12 men sank a hole of 18 feet and struck gold.

10. December 29, 1852

Lyman spoke of visiting travelling companions from Clinton County, Michigan, in Diamond Springs about three miles south of Placerville. He also spoke of a devastating fire in Sacramento. Webster said he was working four miles from Gold Hill (Placer County).

11. January 1, 1853 (Photostat, p. 31)

The letter is headed Michigan Platt Co., Eldorado, California

12. April 29 (1853)

Lyman and five men of his company are aboard the ship Louisa Abrello and are headed for the gold fields of Australia

13. March 2, 1857

Letter to Dimis Webster from her cousin Alvin Bradford of Haydenville, Massachusetts, in which he described the modes of transportation required to traverse the distance between St. Johns, Michigan, and Haydenville, Massachusetts. He inquired of news of Lyman Webster.

14. September 26, 1905

Letter from the Daily Telegraph Newspaper Company, Sydney, Australia, stating they had placed a missing friend notice in their paper.

15. October 13, 1905

A news clip requested information regarding Lyman Webster

Mrs. Ione Anderson related that Lyman Webster wrote home occasionally, stating in a final letter from Australia that he had acquired a large amount of gold and was about to sail for home. That was the last anyone heard about him. (The additional letters have not been located.)

St Joseph we arived here two days ago

May 1th 1850 Dear friends i once more take this opertunity to let you now that i am well at this time and have ben ever since i left home with the exception of a little diane that was caused by the river water i am twelve hundred miles from home now and think of starteing on twesday for the forest i have not seen any sicknes on the rout or herd of none a tall except some few cases of the small pox the most detts that has acured on my rout has been by drinking here is a great marry of the emegrants that do nothing else but drink and gamble one man found dead in a wagon dead with his Jug a side him but the wast nowd that is here would astonish a nation i think that i have seen teams and wagons a nought to reach from texes to pontiac if all compacked and still acomeing they dont make any thing of stabbing a man here amongst the gamblers but dont give your selves any uneasy ness about me because i intend to kep out of all such places i have had now trouble with any man yet there is now feed here yet scarcely but som buy grain to take along untill the feed grows the iamie folks started before i got here all but Dexter and Rindels but i have not seen them yet they lamp out back from the town i rave herd from firk and lucinday they live about forty miles from St lewis they live alone and children with them but the old man does not do any thing they say but drink gits so that he cant get home alone lucinda sweares and lures him but she says there is no one to blame but he .. self we saw a yo any man that has boarded there and she says th he can git him away from him if he pleases we gave him David Richmond name to show to lucinda carl left me at fort independance he got a cha er to go there with a kentucky train but i did not like the train they can yed to many denk nives for me i have come michigan folks here with me i have seen old Balding and came up on the boat from St Lewis with him but he left the boat at fort lanibe but above all the water is the worst here that i ever saw it looks like soap suds any quantity of negrows throu this contry

i want you to get along the best way that you can dont be afraid to get to
Chaunly an you re fatten for hell if you want any but Keep up,
and have my health
good courage if i live i shant come back with out some money if it
in california we shant get there till late becam it will be late before we start
there was sixty men started from here with thirty wheel barrows
and have got half way thrau they say by this time and there
is some astarte ing with hand carts now they change from one to
three hundred dollars to take passengers thrue from here but
we think of packing thrue ~~doing~~ i bought my provision at
St lewis all but dried beef that i got at Chicago i dont know how
things will come out yet but hope that i may have as good luck
as others if i have my health i think that i shall so give
my busens to hellen and Henry and tell all of the Children that
i am agoing to resk my life for there good i dont think of any
more to rite this time idont now as i shall have achance
to wright again un till i get thrau so goodbuy Dimedomen for
this time

my mind is on you all
so take care of your selves
for i am acoming back again

Lyman Webster

it is a harde case to
com loose my mind for there
is sich trouble buruty

Eldorado County California Jan 4th 1851

now I take this oppertunity to drop you a few lines to let
you now that i am well and hearty at this time and
hope these few lines will find you enjoying the same blessing
and your family also and now dont never think of com
ing to California because i tell you the best of the
mining is all dug up here is a man to every rod of ground
all most i was one year to late but i shall stay here
one year from this winter i think now unless we hop on to
some fat place we have got a large quantity of dirt threwe
up but now we have not water yet to wash it out and if we dont
have rain soon we shall leave it till next winter my pard
ners have goan to look out for aa other digings where we can
can get water to wash with they have ben goan one weak
and i am a lone here but on new years day morning i went
down to work about one quarter of a mill to a little crick where
it had ben all dug up amost and i went to work a peeking in
the bank and puked out one lump of one hundred and
six dollars and twenty five cents before noon made some
eight dollars in dust good for new years time but we cant
tell any thing how we have done untill we wash out the
dirt that we have got threw up we had one little rain
so we washed out some three hundred dollars we have
four gold washers and one long tom wear wash more
in one day with the long tom then we can with the
four rockers when we have plenty of water to run it
with but they all cost a power of money we have

Eldorado County letter

28

every thing to do with that we want [illegible] all but
a female to do our cooking i want you to let your mother
see and read it when you get threw with it for i intend to
have one and all see all the letters that i send home but i
have got most out of all hopes of receiving one letter
from any of you while i stay in this place i have sent
some eight letters home and have not one word of
answer from [illegible] of you i would like to now the cause
of it i have [illegible] to a gradeal of trouble i have sent to
the city by the express mail to see if you had sent some
to Sacramento city i wrote the first time to have you
mail youre letters to the city but sence that time
there has been a post office astableshed [illegible] hangtown i sent
in the last letter that i wrote some gold and i want to
now wheather you got it or not i dare not send no
money home unless i have a chance to send it by some
one that i am agnainted with they tell me that it will
not be safe to send by male all that send home send
by some of the friends but wait with patience
for i want to see you all so that i can tell you more then
you ever new you dont now nothing about the world
in Michigan it is as warm here as sum mer all most
we have sot out some unions and they grow fine
they are cheap here onely one dollar a lb las night
i bought five lb of potatoes at 20 cents per lb also two
lbs of butter at one dollar per lb that is the first that
we have had in our house sence we have ben here now i am a
going to rost some potatoes and have some feast with
potatoe and butter i shall make my mouthe go flip a tie
flop

29

— now i will tell you onething about the miners in general they dont any more then one tenth part of them make any more then there board all of the best storys go back to the states and none of the poor ones but i can tell you that it is all luck and chan   'on the gold is in streeks some venry rich and some venry poor i dont now what to rite to you all on the acount of not recieving any   i have told you all about every thing in the letters that   one this one and i must give up the chace soon of heaven   nom you at all but tell all of the children that i think of them ofen and tell them to be good till I shall come back again we have now windws in our house and it is very dank so you must excuse my crooked and bad roynting but i dont think i shall do as well now as i did before i et the great dinner of potatoes and butter for i have fild up to much but never mind i will do the best that i can so i want you all to keep up good pluck un till i come home   a   i will tell you all about the rout and California   i want you to tell me all that has ben agoing on even senze i lift home and about Simon peter magenson Shill who we sent back to have hoockin gandsen meet us to Chigey i heard that he lay as far as St lewis   then returned back again tell him that his pluck was small oh he could done as i did took his pack on his back and foot it throu i went it like one book it was a long road to walk but o the humbolt river but all old and young we traveled on it some sex or seven hundred miles and the water was like alke ly so i must leave you here with my best respects to all both great and small
                                                    Lyman Webster

Michigan platt Co of El adö Califon me

Jan th 18'53

Dear family all I once more take my pen in
hand to inform you that i am well at
this time an Hope these fine lines will
find you all in the same state of health
I do this to let you now that I am in
the land of living yet all though now
friend nonfor takes the pains to send me
one word to me soas to let me now wheathe
you are all dead or not so I thank you
for your pains dont mind about me
I am a diging in a deep bank of dirt
and I can make my grub yet dont be
salarmed about me for i am not dead
yet you will not loos me so quick
    plas send me word wheather
Levey got that money that I sent
to him or not so good by now

    Yours with respects

        Emma Webster

Michigan Platt Co. letter

Transcript of Gold Rush Letters

1. Chicago Ilunois April the 26. 1850
Dear friends i take this opportunity to
pen a few lines to you all that i am well
at present and hope these few lines
will find you the same we have ben
here about one week awaiting for Hill
and gardner we lay by the mouth of
Grand river three days for the convance
a cross the lake then we went aboard
of a steamboat and crarred to millakee
and so all around the rap bush till at last
we arived in Chicago the lake was roughf
as the duse it made me heave and hump
we shall start in to days for St. lewis
if the boys dont come we travel the city
over three or four times a day for them
till we got out of all patience i have
not much news to tell oanly that there was
a steamboat burnt on the missipa and all
lost but the hands most of the passengers
on board was bound for Calafornia last
night we was awoke by the cry of fire
ma youst kiss henry for me and
tell henry to kiss you for me to tell the
boys tʋ keep there heds up for i am a come
ing back again you tell the boys if they want
money to gow to Chauncy and he will
let them have some till i have time
to get back and then will pay up all
hands i have nothing more at present
so i must bid you all goodby but
above all keep your courage up
                                    Lyman Webster

Mr Edwin D Webster
Essex Clinton County
        Mich

(post marked)
      Chicago Ill.
      26 Apr.

2. St Joseph we arrived here two days ago
May 11th 1850 Dear friend i once more take this opportunity to let
you now that i am well at this time and have been well since
I left home with the exsepton of a little diare that was caused
by the river water i am twelve hundred miles from home
now and think of starting on tuesday for the forest i have
not seen any sickness on the mout or head of none a tall except
some few cases of the small pox the most detts that has around
on my mouth as ben by drinking here is a great many of
the emigrants that do nothing else but drink and gamble
one man found dead in a wagon dead with his Jug a side him
but the vast crowd that is here would astonish a nation
i think that i have seen teams and wagons a nough to reach
from Essex to pontiac if all compacted and and still a coming they
don't make any thing of stabbing a man here amongst the
gamblers but dont give your selves any uneasy ness about me
becaus i intend to keep out of all such places i have had now trouble
with any man yet there is now feed here yet scarcely but some
buy grain to take along untill the feed grow the ionia folks
started before i got here all but Dexter and hindes
but i have not seen them yet they camp out back from the
town i have herd from fisk and lucinday they live about
forty miles from St lewis they live alone and children with
them but the old man does not do any thing they say but drink

33

gits so that he cant get home alone lucinda swears and curis him
but she says there is no one to blame but him self we saw a
young man that has boarded there and he says that he can git hur
away from him if he pleases we gave him David Ritchmond name
to show to lucinda Carl left me at fort independence he got
achance to get thrue with a kentucky train but i did not like the train
they caryed to many denk nives for me i have some michigan folks
here with me i have seen old Ralding and came up on the boat
from St Lewis with him but he left the boat at fort Carife but above all
the water is the worst here that i ever saw it looks like
soap suds any quantity of negrows thru this country
i want you to get along the best way that you can don't be afraid to go to
Chauncy or youre father for help if you want any but keep up
good courage if i live and have my health i shant come back
without some money if it
in California we shant get there till late because it will be late before
we start
there are sixty men started from here with thirty wheel barows
and have got half way throu they say by this time and there
is some a starting with hand carts now they charge from one to
three hundred dollars to take passengers thrue from here but
we think of packing there I bought my provisions at
St lewis all but dried beef that i got a Chicago i dont know how
things will come out yet but hope that i may have as good luck
as oathers if i have my health i think that i shall so give
my busens to Hellen and Henry and tell all the children that
i am agoing to risk my life for there good i dont think of any
more to rite this time i dont now as i shall have a chance
to wright again till i get thru so good by Dimadomer for this time

                                        my mind is on you all
                                        so tacare of your selves
it is a harde case to   for i am acoming back again
compose my mind for there
is such hostile country   Lyman Webster

34

Mrs. E. D.Webster
Essex Clinton Co   (post marked)
Michigan   St Joseph Mo
                      May 14

3. Direct your letter to Placer vill or Hangtown
California December the 8th 1850 Eldorado County
I take one more opportunity to let you now that i am in the
land of the living yet and that my health is good and hope these
few lines will find you all well at home i have not heard
one word from one of you sense i left home and this is the sixth
letter that i have rote home sense i left i want you should
send letters as often as you can make it convenient to and let
me now how you are all get along at home and all about every
thing and every boddy around there i dont now as you have
received one letter from me sense i left home i have sent some
of them to the city by men that are going down and sent the
money by them to pay the postage and i want you should let
me now wheather you have received them or not and wheather
the postage was paid om it i shall go to the office myself
with this letter and see that it is mailed and pay the postage
you may not look for me home till one year from next spring
becuas i dont think it would look well for me to come so far and
(?) my legs off for nothing the chance for mineing and . . .
farm and i will bring you a play thing Hellen you must be the
pretty girl amongst the hole crowd Henry I want you to take
good care of your calf and be a good boy and I will bring you a
little Spanish girl so i must leave you all in the hands of your maker
i have no more time to rite at this time the last
letter that i sent I sent to Theodore but i intend them to you
all as one I want to see you all as bad as can be but the (?)time will
soon roll around if i should stay one year longer so good by . . .
send home some money to him if we can have rain so we can

work it out we have not much on hand now but soon can have
When the rain comes because we have the stuff threw up
we have not done anything sense the third day of October
but to throw up dirt on the account of water we have panned
out some to try it as we went along so as to tell weather it
would pay or not but we hapto to gow a quarter of a mile to
water but have some very good pans of dirt (?) bigest
pan full that we paned out we got fourteen dollars gold out
of one pan of dirt but it was an accident because we found one lump
that was over thirteen dollars and now i send a specimen of what
we are a digging out of the earth the largest peaces that you
will find ways sixty three cents and the five i did not way i only
send it as a specimen to let you now how it looks when thinking
of what i am about i dont intend to fool away my time
while i am in this lomesome hole we have been here a going on
three months and I have not been to Hangtown in the hole time
but have been to weaver town some three times after provisions
but i can tell you that we stick clost to our work Dewey i want
you to do the best that you can until i come home again and will see
that you are well
which i shall do if my life is spared we have the same keepre . . .

Mrs Dimis Webster
Essex Clinton County
Michigan

4. Eldorado Count California Jan 4th, 1851
now i take this opportunity to drop you a few lines to let
you now that i am well and hearty at this time and
hope these few lines will find you enjoying the same blessings
and your family also and dont never think of coming
to California because i tell you that the best of the
mining is all dug up there is a man to every rod of ground
all most i was one year to late but i shall stay here

one year from this winter i think now unles we hap. . . on to
some fat place we have got a large quantity of dirt threwed
up but now water yet to wash it out and if we dont
have rain soon we shall leave it till next winter my pand
men have goan to look out for another diging where we
can get water to wash with they have been goan one week
and i am alone here but on new years day morning went
down to work about one quarter of a mile to a little creek
it had been all dug up amost and i went to work a polking in
the bank and took out one lump of one hundred and
six dollars and twenty five cents before noon made some
eight dollars in dust good for new years to me but we cant
tell anything how we have done untill we wash out the
dirt that we have got threwed up we had one little rain
so we washed out some three hundred dollars we have
four good washers and one long tom then we can wash more
in one day with the long tom then we can with the
four rockers when we have plenty of water to run it
with but they all cost a lot of money we have
every thing to do with that we want here all but
a female to do our cooking i want you to let your mother
see and read it when you get threw with it for i intend
to have one and all see all the letters i send home but i
have got most out of hopes of receiving one letter
from any of you while i stay in this place i have sent
some eight letters and i have not one word of
answer one sole of you i would like to now the cause
of it i have been to a gra deal of trouble i have sent to
the City by the Express mail to see if you had sent some
to Sacramento i wrote the first time to have you
mail your letters to the citty but sense that time
there has been a post office astablished at hangtown i sent
in the last letter that i rote some gold and i want to
now wheather you got it or not i dare not send no
money home unless i have a chance to send it by some

one that i am aquainted with they tell me that it will
not be safe to send by male all that send home send
by some of their friends but wait with patience
for i want to see you all so that i can tell you more then
you ever new you dont now nothing about the world
in Michigan it is as warm here as summer all most
we have sat out some onions and they grow fine
they are cheap here only one dollar a lb last night
I bout five lb of potatoes at 20 cents per lb also too
lbs of butter at one dollar per lb that is the first that
we have had in our house sense we have been here now i am a
going to rost some potatoes and have some feast with
potatoes and butter it shall make my mouth go flip and flop
now i will tell you sonthing about the miners in general
they dont any more then one tenth part of them
make any more then there board all the best storys go back
to the states and none of the poor ones but i can tell you that
it is all luck and chance for the gold is in streaks some very
rich and some very poor i dont now what to rite you a
all on the account of not receiving any from you i have told
you all about every thing in the letters thats sent before this one
and i must give up the thou soon of hearing from you at
all but tell all the children that i think of them orfen
and tell them to be good till i shall come back again
we have now windows in our house and it is very dark so
you must excuse my crooked and bad righting but
i dont think i shall as well now as i did before i et the
great dinner of potatoes and butter for i have fild up to
much but never mind i will do the best that i can so
i want you all to keep up good pluck until i come home
and the i will tell you all about the nort and California
i wont you you to tell me all that has been a going on ever sense
i left home and about Simon Peter Magenson Hill
who we sent back to have Hoocker gardner meet us to Chicago
I heard that he came as far as St Lewis and then returned

38

back again tell him his pluck was small or he could
done as i did took his pack on his back and foot it through
i went it like one book it was a long road to walk but
o the humbolt river but all old and young we traveled
on it some six or seven hundred miles and the water was like
alke ly so i must leave you here with my best respects to all
both great and small   Lyman Webster

Mr Hiram Richmond
Essex Clinton Co
Michigan

5.   Niles Michigan
                           Nov 20 1852
Mrs Demis Webster
                  Your Husband
Mr Lyman Webster Sent a Draft
of $300 by E Taylor from California
to you he has gone to Indiana and
left the Draft with me subject to
your order Mr Webster requested
him to write you and have you
send for the draft here but I can
send it in a letter by mail
if you wish it Please write and
instruct me.
                  Respectfully Yours
                  S W Griffins

6. Sunit River Feb 15, 1852
I do . . . I am tuff and well now
Dear wife I once more have the opportunity of addressing a
few lines to you and the children hopeing that these will find

you all injoying the same blessings I received your letter
the 18 of Feb just 2 months from the time it was mailed
this is the first word that I have heard from any
of you sense i left home it made me feel good to heare
from you and heare that you are all well but youre
self I hope you will be careful of your self i think of
you all and have prayed for you all when on my
loanly bunk I lay knight after knight i have
lain and thought of you all you told me in youre
letter that you was afraid that if i stayed much longer
I would forget to come home but you need not think
that of me I think to much about home you may depend
but I thought as long as i was here I might as well as stay a spell
longer for the benifitt of our family you need not think
it be mutch pleasure for me to stay here adiging
amongst the rocks unless it was for our interest to do so
we have not had but a little rain here yet so we are bothered
to death for water in our revein that we are to work on
the name of the revein is Kioty that we work on now
They is but three of us in Com now there was one more
but we could not do any thing with him so we bought
him out and we live as happy as anyboddy can in our
situation we have a good tent with a fli over it all the
trouble is it is most to warm we have got potatoes up
and big enough to howe that we planted in January
I think that you may look for me next fall if alive to
return we have not done anything with our grants
yet we are awaiting for the machine to get in goo work
ing order and then we shall prospect our grants as i told you
in my other letter we have some of the bigest bugs in
the citty to see us about the grants the officers met at
our tent the oather knight and we greed to wait a while
longer yet before we went into operation yet we mean
to go on the shure side I want you to tell Hellen and
Henry that I will give them one good smugling when i

come tell Dewey that i shall get the art of
working the Cradle very well and by the time
that i come home i expect to find a lump to rock tell
him I wish them much Joy but whare is Theodore
you must of forgot to toold me about them i want to
now how they all get along this world is a filling up
with eastern peopple the fastest you ever saw thirteen
hundred people arrived by steamer and the papers state
that the Ismus is runing over with emergrants that
are awaiting passage but i guess they will wish
themselves back again the stages gow fool to the brimm
I thought that I would rigght one letter without being disturbed
but to my astonishment the tent was filled with men so dont
blame me if it rong side up some of them are a
whining because they cant make no money but the
reason is is because they whiskey to well It wont do for
men to drink if they want to get any gold of any amount
but I dont mean to have that case with me

7. Sunit Diggins California April 25, 1852
Dear Wife I once more take this opportunity to let you
now that i am well and hope these few lines will find you
and the children all well this is the 21 letter that i have
rote you and the boys and have not received but one from
you all and told me in that letter that you had not
received but to from me I paid the postage on all the
to or three and i paid it to the Express men that go thru
the mines and it cost from one to five dollars to get them
carryed to the Cithy and I suspect that they do not put these
in to the office but keep the money and throw the letters away
for I am not the only one that dont get there letters so dont
blaim me for it i have sent some money by one letter
(?) and you said nothing about it and I have got some now
that I wish you had but have no chance to send it safe

but if you want some send word and i will risk it
by mail once more I dont now weather i shall come
home this fall or not but if I shall shure come in the
last of winter if my life is spared i dont now but I
shall go to the City tomorrow if not to of our
boys is going down and I shall send this by them and send
by the express from mine to the states it will only cost
*** to send it by the Express but dont fail to sending
*** weather you want you want some money or not by
*** home or not I have just returned from
*** tains on a prospecting voyge and left snow
*** foot deep on the mountains one dutchman
*** with me we went on horse back and we intend
*** this weeak we form company today to our
tent of twelve men and they are to pay there
the expences on the excertion in the mountains now i will
leave this and come to some other point you may think
I dont care anything about home but you may
not think so for there is not one day nor one hour but
what I think of you all and even to be with you all
but I came a great distance for a little money and i think
it not best to go home empty but this country does not agree
with the news you get in the states times are hard
for California we could do very well where we are now for
we had the water but our water has failed and we are obliged
to go to another diggins so we are a going to Tirtle Hill on
the South fork of the north fork of the American River
and Mazury Canion we intend to summer in that
Canion There will be 12 of us in Company dont blame
me if me if i dont rite a long yarn i have sent so many
long ones to you and you have not got one of them and it
makes me most mad dont poak fun at my senatting
because my hands are very stiff and lazy handleing the
shovel and peck so much I have been down to town this
morning to change some of my dust for gold coin but

could not find but seventy dollars in coins got one
dollar peace and to penny it is handyer to carry a bill
*** dust so i will leave that I want you to
*** what for a trade you have made in swap
*** and tell me who had or to have boot tell my
*** daughter that I am a coming to see hur one
*** ask Dewey if i shall bringe one of our
home with me it might be that he would rock
*** dirt with it it is a very fine one
I want you to send me word how you get along and
every thing that is a going on in town give my love
and best respects to all the children tell henry and helen
i want to see them bad and tell henry I will tell him
goo storys when i come home there is some men
hung all most every week if a man steals fifty dollars
he is shure to be hung I dont think you will care to read
much more of my lingo I think i will leave of by saying
good by for the time but my best respects to all
both great and small This from youre husband
                                            Lyman Webster

8.   San Francisco May 31, 1852
Mrs Webster
Madam
Your husband is at work at a
place called Mt Greyby near the
middle fork of the American river eighty
miles about Sac City when I left him
one week since in good health and
enjoying himself fine by judging from
his appearance and conversation he has
been there a short time but thinks
he will do first-rate he is with a
company of twenty men all good and jolly

43

fellows as he tells me
     I write these few lines
by his request it not being convenient
for him to write you at this time I sent
it by Express as directed
               Respectfully
               M Nodges

Mrs Demis Webster
Essex Clinton Co
    Michigan

9.   Tirtle Hill California June the 10 1852
I now take this opportunity to let you now that
I am well and as tuff as a dried owl and hope these
lines will fine you In Joying the same blessings i received
youre letter in six weeks from date and was happy
to hear that you was all well you told me that you
wanted me to send you some money to pay for the
west Eighty and i had sent a draft of one hundred
dollars before i received you letter and then i sent
another draft of one hundred and if that goes safe
i want you to send me word as quick as you receive
this letter and tell me how much you want sent before
i come home it will be about fall wheather i come
home before next spring or not but if i live until
then i shall come then i want you to tell me wheather
the hubbells farm is sold or not and the price and
let me now how Theodore gets along and about
his health i have now nuse to tell you now
but i will tell you a little about what we are
doing i am in company with 11 men that makes
twelve in our company we are to work in a
canion where we cant but just look out we dont

now how we shall make out yet but we took out
five hundred and six dollars last week out of one
hole that we sunk wee goed about 18 feet deep
before we struck the gold some we dont find any
Tell henry that i want to see him very bad
and all the rest of the family i have now respects
of the children but i have got some peaces
of gold fir you all that will make you all
laugh i have some for all of you to let you now
how it looks as we dig it out of the ground so i cant
say no more now Dimis Keep up good Courage. . .
for i am coming back again my mind is not
off of you long to time i can tell you so much i must. . .
leave you give my best respects to all
inquiring friends

                         From youre father
                         Lyman Webster

10. California Dec the 29, 1852
Dear wife I once more take this opportunity to let
you now that I am well and hope these few lines
will find you injoying the same blessings I long
to here from you once more and hope that i shall
hear from you are all well I have not had but
one letter from you sense i left home and one from
Dewey and Robert but you need not look for
many more from me whilst i stay here
because i intend to come home between this and the
fourth of July next if my life is spared i wish
you would send me one letter before I leave
and send weather you have got the drafts
that i sent to you by mail or not and the
gane tipe that i sent to you or not and all about
(?) everything else i was over to Dimond springs

the other day and saw Milo Turner and family
and young Stuart House and Robert Mc
Ru Jesse Foot Turner is in the city of Sacromento
and the city is all burnt up and it makes
provisions very high in the mines pork is worth
about one hundred dollars per barrell and flower
fifty to the barrel and anything else is addition
I wrote to Dewey and told him to send to me wheather
he wanted more money before i come home on
but have not had any answer yet do please send
me one more letter if you do pleas and i will buss
you when i come home to pay for it you
must not laugh at my righting for i am arighting by
candle light and it bothers me to follow the lines
tell the children that i want to see them all and tell
henry i want to heare him stutter once more
and Hellen to dont now as is much use tonight much
because i dont get much from you but will Just
send to let you now that i am alive and well
i hope you all get along well and tuff now dont
forget to right as quick as you receive this it has
just comensed raining and it rains most all the time
Lorenzo Dexter works at gold hill about four miles from
where i am to work but i have not seen him but heard
from him the other day I understood that Pitts had
goan home last fall but i shall stay here till the
water fails in the spring and peck away Can't make
much more because California is all dug over and over
so i will leave you by telling you that i went to a
wild bull and grissaly bear fight the other day
Sunday and bull tore the beare all to pieces
but there is one thing more there were four men
went out the other day and to hunt a grisely and
one of them got all tore to peases it was about one
mile from where we are to work I dont think

of anything that will be interesting to you so
I will leave you not long i hope this from your

                    Dearest Husband
                    Lyman Webster

11. Michigan Platt Co of Eldorado California
Jan the 1 1853
Dear family all I once more take my pen in
hand to inform you that i am well at
this time and hope these few lines will
find you all in the same state of health
I do this to let you now that I am in
the land of living yet all though now
friend nor foe takes the pains to send me
one word to me so as to let me now wheather
you are all dead or not so I thank you
for youre pains dont mind about me
I am a diging in a deep bank of durt
and can make my grubs yet dont be
alarmed about me for i am not dead
yet you will not loos me so quick
Pleas send me word wheather
Dewey got the money that I sent
to him or not so good by now
        Your's Withe respect
        Lyman Webster

12. Last letter written before sailing for Australia (probably 1853)

San Francisco April 29 th
Dear wife and children all I once more
take my pen in hand to inform you that
I am well and hope these few lines will find

47

you all enjoying the same blessing I do expect
that you will be alarmed about the voige that
I am about to take we start tomorrow for
Australia it is eight thousand miles from here
but I can send letters from there as quick as from
California and if I live to get there i will right
to you and tell you all where to send youre letters
I have five men with me that i have ben to work
with a long time One is from Michigan one from Ilanois
and the other from indiana They came out in fifty
the same year that i came but we dont mean to stay
very long in the mines there I have not had but
three letters from you all since i left home not heard
from the money that I sent except the first but
I hope you got it all Dewey I want you to do the
best that you can until i come home and youre
mother and brothers and sisters all well
I know that it is a task for you but i hope you will
have youre pay bovit and you will if i live
to return again I am aboard the Louisa Abellsan
about one hundred and fifty passengers about
you need not think i do not want to see you all
because I do not one hour day nor knight but
think of you all but I hope and I trust that we
will meat again in this world dont be down hearted
any of you because I think it is the best for me
to go there according to all the acounts from
there I will rite a long letter when i get to
Australia if i am lucky anough to get there
you must not blame me for not righting a long
letter because this boat is in a great confusion now
and i and I cant bring my thoughts to geather
and so i must leave off by biding you all good by
for this time
  This from your husband and father Lyman Webster

13. Letter from Alvin Bradford

        Haydenville Hamphire

        March 2nd, 1857

Dear cousin if I mistake not I agreed to wright
to you after my return Mass I have delayed
for some time but will now indeavoir to fulfill the enjoyment
We had a fine ride from your place to St Johns got
there in time to take the stage for Owasso had a very
bad driver & bad ride however we indured the ride
got there in time to take the cars & glad were we
had a fine ride to Detroit arrived there about 6 we
we thence we went on board a steamer for Cleveland
started out about 7 o'clock Eve arrived at Cleveland soon
after daylight had a fine ride we then took a carriage
& was soon landed at the door of Mr Parish had a fine
visit with them. I left my wife with them & started
the next morn being Saturday went to Hinkley found
uncle Wait & Emily well and in comfortable circunstances
I visited Horace Wait found them well and comfortably situated
Irene Likewise in prosperous circumstances. I remained at H-
until the next Wednesday morn I left for Cleveland in
company with Uncle Wait got to C- early in the morn
in the Pm we took carriage in company with Emerancy. Emerancy
went to Newburgh my former place of residence visited the
cemetry found that sacred spot where the remains of
dear Abby lies. I could not help from lingering about that
spot for some time. Newburgh has altered considerable since
I left Cleveland is a large city the next morn thursday
about 8 o'clock we took the cars for the East a butifull morn
on we went in fine spirits & with good luck we arrived
at Buffalo about 5 pm changed cars & on we went with
great rappidity got to Rochester a distance of about 90 miles
from B- before quite dark & on we came through the Knight
early in the morning we were at Albany we had
breakfast & soon crosst the river & took the cars again for

Springfield thenc to Northampton & from Northampton
to Haydenville & glad were we we found our place &
things in good shape we had a fine fall for crops for busing
Dece was not very severe Jan was extremely cold Feb quite mild
Cousin in regards to the old place i cannot say anything more than
I said to you while at your place. time with us is fast passing
away. it will be said of us that we have gone the way of all
the earth. your friends as far as I know are all well. the family
of Mrs Lawrence are well and doing well. they took it very
kind in Theodore in sending his minature & said that they
would like to see him & all the rest of the family.
I have had a letter from Mr and Mrs Price saying that they
had the pleasure of a visit fron you I think it was
very gratifying to Sis F likewise they inform me of their
visit this winter to your place which was very peasing I think
it will have a tendance to make Fidelin more contended with
her situation. I hope you will visit them as often as you can
we have often thought of the time we spent with you & your
children which was very pleasing very indeed. we would
like to renew the visit at some future day but that is uncertain
we would be glad to have a visit from you or some of your children. things with
us are very high flour 5 to 10 per bil
corn 85 to 90 potatoes 75 cts pork in the hog 11 cts beef 7.8
butter 25 cheese 12 1/2 eggs 25 cts per doz stock very high
over that will weigh 3,000 - 1.50 cows according to quality
30-40-50 to 75 I have one that I have been offered 65 price 70
The stock in proportion hay 12-14 I have thought some
of disposing of my property & spending some time at the west
but that is not certain Cousin now I am about to close
by wishing & yours health all the prosperity that is best
for mortals to injoy now cousin will you wright to
me & give me as perticulars as I have you give me
the perticulars about your house and barn & stock & farm and all your
children & whether you have heard from Mr Webster if so
if you get tired of wrighting let some of the rest wright

I shall be glad to here any thing & all about the west
wen you wright please direct to Haydenville

Hamphere

Mass

yours with many sespects

Alvin Bradford

Haydenville March 2 nd, 1857

14. Daily Telegraph Newspaper Company Limited

Sydney September 26 th 1905

Mr. L. Parr.

Box. 368

St Johns. Michigan. U.S.A.

Dear Sir,

We received your letter of August 2, asking us to insert
Missing Friends Notice re Lyman Webster in our paper, and in com-
pliance with your wishes we published the announcement in our issues
of Saturday last and to-day, at a cost of 5/- per insertion, 10/- for
the two. (2 dollars 50 cents.) We shall be glad to receive Post
Office Order from you for the amount at your kind convenience. Trusting
the insertion of the notice will be successful in securing the information desired.

Yours faithfully.

The Daily Telegraph Newspaper

Co.

15. Newspaper clipping   10/13/05

Webster, Lyman, who sailed from San Francisco in
the ship Louisa Abrello, about 1852, for Sydney
One letter was received from him after his arrival,
but he has not been heard of since. He was a gold
miner in California, and left with a party of
three or four mates for the gold diggins in Australia.

If now alive would be about 90 years of age. Any
information regarding him or relatives in NSW will
be thankfully received by his grandson L. D. Parr
Box 368 St Johns, Mich. USA.

The Webster Family

Several members of Lyman Webster's family settled in central Michigan.
His oldest sister, Anna Webster Sadler, died at Tecumseh, Michigan. Chester
Webster, seventh generation descendent of John Webster, was born June 13,
1795. He and his wife, Polly, were among the early settlers in Oakland County,
Michigan. Chester's first son, John, and his wife, Chloe, moved to Bath Town-
ship, Clinton County, in 1867 and purchased land in Section 8, now 12812
Webster Road.

Edwin Dewey Webster was born in Franklin County, Massachusetts,
October 26, 1828, and died in his home in Essex Township, Clinton County,
Michigan, September 5, 1896, from the effects of paralysis.

He was the second son of Lyman and Dimis (Stebbins) Webster. Dewey
was six when his parents came to Michigan, settled in Kent County, and erected
a sawmill at or near Grand Rapids. This was the year 1834. They remained
there a short time, then moved to Ionia County, where they resided until 1837,
when they came to Clinton County. They settled on what was afterwards
known as the "Webster Prairie," and later known as the "Rolfe Farm."
Dewey married Elizabeth Parr, December 25, 1851. Two children were born,
Mary D. Webster (Casterline) and Elizabeth M. Webster (Casterline). They
settled on a farm two miles east of Maple Rapids, Michigan. While residing
there his wife, Elizabeth, sickened and died April 27, 1855. In the year 1858,
Dewey purchased 120 acres of improved land which he transformed into a hand-
some farm. On September 12 of the same year, he married Caroline Weller,
sister of Andrew Weller of Bengal township. They had no children.

Photographs

1. Lyman Webster
2. Dimis Stebbins Webster
3. Edwin Dewey Webster, third child of Lyman
4. Edwin Dewey Webster
5. Caroline Weller Webster, second wife of Dewey
6 Caroline Weller Webster
7. Henry Ware Webster, tenth child of Lyman
8. Caroline Webster Randolph, sixth child of Lyman
9. Louisa Webster Baker, fifth child of Lyman
10. Lyman's sister
11. Lyman's sister's husband
12. Emma Thayer Waters (Winters), Dewey's cousin. Her parents were Sarah A. Webster and Horace Stebbins Thayer of Conway, Massachusetts.
13. Carla Anderson sitting on a primitive rocker once owned by Dimis Webster. She is the great, great, great, great granddaughter of Lyman Webster. (1989 photo)
14. Red brick farm house, Clinton County, Michigan, purchased in 1875 by Dewey Webster. (1989 photo)
15. Large red barn; same property as in 14. Built 1879. (1989 photo)

1. Lyman Webster

2. Dimis Stebbins Webster

3. Edwin Dewey Webster,
third child of Lyman

4. Edwin Dewey Webster

5. Caroline Weller Webster,
second wife of Dewey

6. Caroline Weller Webster

7. Henry Ware Webster,
tenth child of Lyman

8. Caroline Webster Randolph,
sixth child of Lyman

9. Louisa Webster Baker,
fifth child of Lyman

10. Lyman's sister

11. Lyman's sister's husband

12. Emma Thayer Waters (Winters), Dewey's cousin. Her parents were
Sarah A. Webster and Horace Stebbins Thayer of Conway, Massachusetts.

13. Carla Anderson is the great, great, great, great granddaughter of
Lyman and Dimis Webster. She resides in Clinton County, Michigan.
The rocker she is sitting on, the small hand mirror she is holding in
her hand, and the chest in the background were brought by the Websters
from Massachusetts in 1834.

The rocker to the right of Carla was the same one Caroline Webster sat
in when a drunken Indian picked up a hatchet from a woodpile and threw
it through the window of the Websters' home, barely missing the head of
the child. The Indian was angered because Dimis had not let him come
in; she had not wanted him to walk across her newly-mopped floor.

14. Red brick farm house, Clinton County, Michigan, purchased in 1875 by Dewey Webster (1989 photo)

15. Large red barn; same property as in 14. Built 1879 (1989 photo).

The Webster Family Genealogy

Gov. John Webster
b. 1590 England
d. Apr. 5, 1661
Hartford, Ct.

Lt. Robt. Webster   m. England
b. 1627 England   Agnes Shotwell
d. May 31, 1676   d. 1667
Hartford, Ct.   Hadley, Ma.

Dea. Jon. Webster   m. 1652
b. Jan. 9, 1656   Susannah Treat
Middletown, Ct.   b. 1629
d. 1735   d. 1705

Jonathan Webster   m. May 11, 1681   Hartford, Ct.
b. Mar. 18, 1681   Dorcas Hopkins
d. Sept. 18, 1758   d. 1695 Hartford
Hartford, Ct.   m. Jan. 2, 1696   Stephen Webster
m. Dec. 14, 1704   Mary Judd   b. June 11, 1728
Esther Judd   d. Feb. 4, 1818
b. Feb. 8, 1686   Northfield, Ma.
d. Dec. 22, 1782   Jacob Webster   m. Glastonbury, Ct.
  Bernardston, Ma.   b. Feb. 12, 1748   RebeckahWilliams
                                     Glastonburg, Ct.   b. Hartford, Ct.
                                     d. Oct. 3, 1776   d. Oct. 8, 1766
                     Jacob Webster   While in Army   m. Dec. 2, 1767
                     b. July 23, 1772 m. May 13, 1770   Glastonbury, Ct.
                     Bernardston, Ct. Wethersfield, Ct.   Elizabeth Fox
                     d. Feb. 15, 1847 Abigail Goodrich   d. Dec. 20, 1787
Lyman Webster   Housatonic, Ma.   m. 1788
b. Feb. 8, 1803   m. 1792   Northfield, Ma.
Franklin Co., Ma.   Lovina Hemingway   Patience Johnson
d. 1856?   b. Feb. 10, 1773   d. Aug. 1809
Australia   Farmington, Ct.   Northfield, Ma.
m. Feb. 10, 1825   d. June 11, 1845
Dimis Stebbins   Curtesville, Ma.
Clinton Co., Mi.

The Stebbins Genealogy
(forebears of Dimis , who
married Lyman Webster)

Rowland Stebbins
b. 1594 England
d. Dec. 14, 1671

John Stebbins
b. 1626 England
d. Mar. 7, 1678
Northampton, Ma.
m. in England to
Sarah
b. 1591 England
d. Oct. 1649
Springfield, Ma.

John Stebbins
b. Jan 28, 1647
Springfield, Ma.
d. Dec. 19, 1724
Deerfield, Ma.
m. Dorothy Alexander

m. Ann (Munson)
   widow
d. 1656 Springfield, Ma.

John Stebbins
b. about 1687
d. Sept. 7, 1760
m. (1st) about 1714
Mary
m. (2nd) about Aug. 1735
Hannah Allen
b. Feb. 12, 1698

David Stebbins son of John b. 1687
by second marriage
b. Apr. 20, 1741 Deerfield, Ma.
d. Sept. 30, 1816 Conway, Ma.
m. Dec.18, 1765
Rhoda Sheldon
b. Oct. 24, 1748 Deerfield, Ma.
d. Aug. 8, 1826 Conway, Ma.

Chester Stebbins
b. July 22, 1778
d. July 18, 1848
Ionia, Mi.
m. Jan. 7, 1802
Nancy Burroughs
b. Feb. 10, 1787
d. Aug. 5, 1848
Ionia, Mi.

(David was a lieutenant, and Rhoda's
brother, Abner, was a sergeant in the
Revolutionary War)

Dimis Stebbins
b. May 10, 1804
Franklin Co., Ma.
d. Nov. 28, 1875
Clinton Co., Mi.
m. Feb. 10, 1825
Lyman Webster

The Burroughs Genealogy
Maternal Forebears of Dimis Webster

Ebenezer Burroughs born July 1, 1753
His wife Anne Easton born Sept. 30, 1759
They were married July 1, 1778
their first child was born Dec.11, 1778
their second child Charlotte was born June 11, 1780
their third child George was born Nov. 24, 1782
their fourth child Ebenezer was born Aug. 10, 1784
their fifth child Nancy was born Feb. 10, 1787 (Dimis Webster's mother)
their sixth child Lucy was born Feb. 11, 1789
their seventh child Joel was born Sept. 20, 1791
their eight child Anne was born Aug. 25 ,1793
their ninth child Polly was born Oct. 26, 1795
their tenth child Seth was born April 10 ,1800
their eleventh child Polly was born May 15, 1802
their twelfth child born May 15, 1803

their first child died Dec. 13, 1778, age 28 hours
their eighth child Annie died Feb. 4, 1795
their ninth child Polly died Nov. 4, 1797
their third child George died July 21, 1801
their fourth child Ebenezer died Aug 4, 1820
Joel died Feb. 27, 1826
Charlotte died January 17, 1828
Seth died April 10, 1828
Ebenezer Burroughs died Oct. 27, 1828
His wife Anne died June 26, 1839, in the 80th year of her age

References

Clinton: File of the Clinton County clerks's office, St. Johns, Michigan

Clinton: History of Bath Charter Township, Clinton County, Michigan, 1826-1976, by Harold B. Burnett, printed and bound by Owosso Graphics Art, 1976.

Clinton: History of Clinton County, Michigan, published by the Clinton County Historical Society, St. Johns, Michigan, 1980, pages 7, 302.

Clinton: Past and Present of Clinton County, Michigan, by Judge S. B. Dabott, Chicago, the S. J. Clarke Publ. Co., 1905, pages 468, 469.

Clinton: Portrait, Biological Album of Clinton and Shiawassee Counties, Michigan, Chicago, Chapman Bro., 1891, p. 970

Grand River: Memorials of the Grand River Valley by Franklin Everett, Chicago, the Chicago Legal News Co., 1879, page 51.

Ionia: History of Ionia and Montcalm Counties, Michigan by John S. Schneck, Philadelphia, D. W. Ensign & Co., 1881, page 114.

Ionia: Plat Map, Ionia County, Michigan, sponsored by Ionia Co. 4-H Leaders Council, Publ. Rockford Map Co., Rockford, Illinois, 1967, page 23.

Ionia: Atlas of Ionia County, Michigan, F. W. Beers & Co., New York, 1875.

Kent: Federal Land Patents, Kent County, Michigan, Western Genealogical Society of Grand Rapids, Michigan, 1984, page 67.

Kent: Kent County, Michigan Land Records, Michigan Works Progress Administration, Vital Records Project, Michigan State Library & D.A.R., Grand Rapids, Michigan, 1940. Vol. 5, page 1426.

Kent: 1841 Plat Map, Grand Rapids Township, Kent County, Michigan.

Massachusetts: Vital Records of Conway, Massachusetts to the Year 1850, Publ. New England Historical Genealogical Society, Boston, Massachusetts, 1943, pages 96, 106, 187, 195, 264, 269.

Openlander: Personal recollections and photographs, Mrs. Jean Anderson Openlander.

Shiawassee: History of Shiawassee and Clinton Counties, Michigan, Philadelphia, D. W. Ensign & C., 1880, pages 341, 398, 399, 450, 475.

Stebbins: The Stebbins Genealogy (2 volumes) by Ralph Stebbins Greenlee and Robert Lemuel Greenlee, Chicago, Illinois, 1904, page 315.

Webster: History and Genealogy of the Gov. John Webster Family of Connecticut, William Holcomb Webster and Rev. Melville Reuben Webster, DD, Rochester, New York, 1915, pages 909-918.